REAL LIFE SEA MONSTERS

Stingrays

by Ruth Owen

PowerKiDS
press™

New York

Published in 2014 by The Rosen Publishing Group, Inc.
29 East 21st Street, New York, NY 10010

Produced for Rosen by Ruby Tuesday Books Ltd
Editor for Ruby Tuesday Books Ltd: Mark J. Sachner
US Editor: Joshua Shadowens
Designer: Emma Randall

Photo Credits:
Cover, 1, 6–7, 8–9, 16–17, 24–25, 26–27 © Shutterstock; 4–5, 9 (top),
12–13 © FLPA; 10–11, 14 © Alamy; 15, 18–19 © Superstock; 20–21 ©
Jean-Francois Helias; 23 © Zeb Hogan; 28–29 © Wikipedia
Creative Commons.

Library of Congress Cataloging-in-Publication Data

Owen, Ruth, 1967–
Stingrays / by Ruth Owen.
     pages cm. — (Real life sea monsters)
Includes index.
ISBN 978-1-4777-6265-3 (library) — ISBN 978-1-4777-6266-0 (pbk.) —
ISBN 978-1-4777-6267-7 (6-pack)
1. Stingrays—Juvenile literature. I. Title.
QL638.8O94 2014
597.3'5—dc23
                                         2013029245

Manufactured in the United States of America

CPSIA Compliance Information: Batch #W14PK7: For Further Information contact: Rosen Publishing, New York, New York at 1-800-237-9932

CONTENTS

BEAUTIFUL AND DEADLY

For hundreds of years, sailors told stories of sea serpents and giant beasts that lurked deep beneath the ocean.

Today, we know these monsters do not exist. The world's oceans are home, however, to many incredible and, sometimes, enormous creatures. Huge whales, fearsome sharks, and giant **predatory** fish swim, hunt, and raise their young in waters around the world.

One such creature moves through water like a giant, underwater bird. It is armed with a lethal weapon, and can kill an enemy with its powerful **venom**. It is graceful, beautiful, but potentially deadly. This real life sea monster is the stingray.

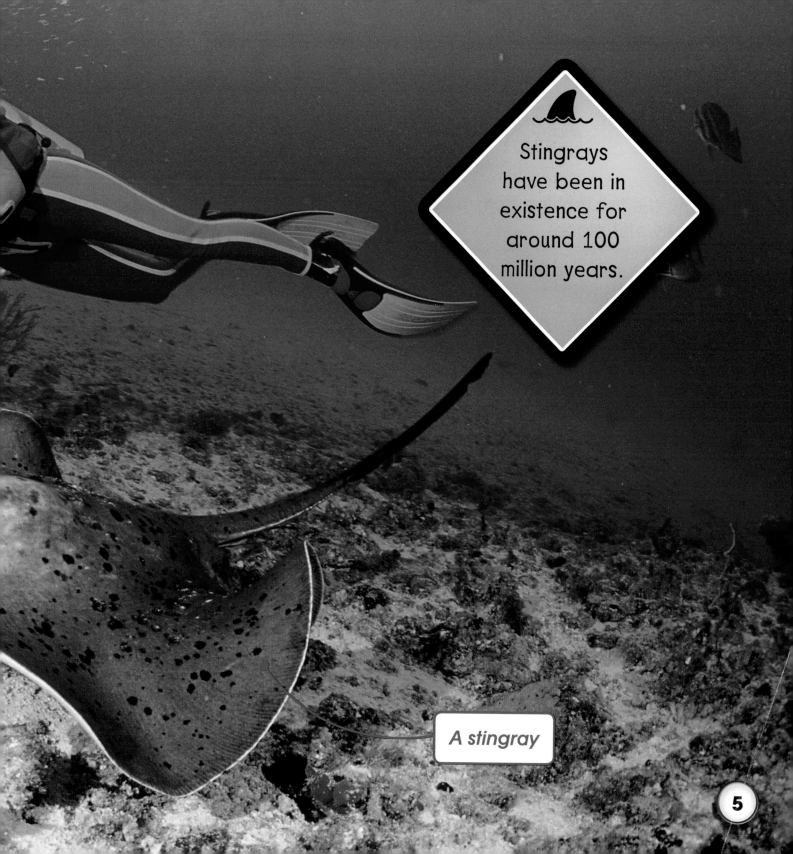

Stingrays have been in existence for around 100 million years.

A stingray

WHAT ARE STINGRAYS?

Rays are fish that live both in oceans and in freshwater places, such as rivers.

The ray family includes many different **species**. Some of the most fascinating are the many types of stingrays, the enormous manta ray, and the truly electrifying electric rays, creatures that use electricity to kill their victims!

Rays have flat, often rounded, bodies that contain no bones. Instead of bones, a ray's body is supported by **cartilage**, the same material that forms the hard, but rubbery, parts of your ears.

Stingrays usually live in warm, shallow waters close to shorelines. Most types of stingrays spend their lives partly buried in sand on the seabed, hiding from **predators** and waiting to catch **prey**.

A blue spotted stingray

Stingrays and the other members of the ray family are related to sharks.

A stingray buried in sand

PHYSICAL FACTS

Like all fish, stingrays have fins. Their wide fins run the full length of their bodies, creating their rounded shapes.

When they swim, some rays move their whole bodies in an undulating, wave-like motion. Other types flap their fins like a bird's wings and look as if they are flying through the water.

Stingrays come in many different sizes. Some species are just 12 inches (30 cm) long. Large species can grow to 6.5 feet (2 m) long, including their tails, and almost 6 feet (1.8 m) wide. These stingray giants may weigh more than 700 pounds (318 kg).

A southern stingray swimming

Fin

Eyes

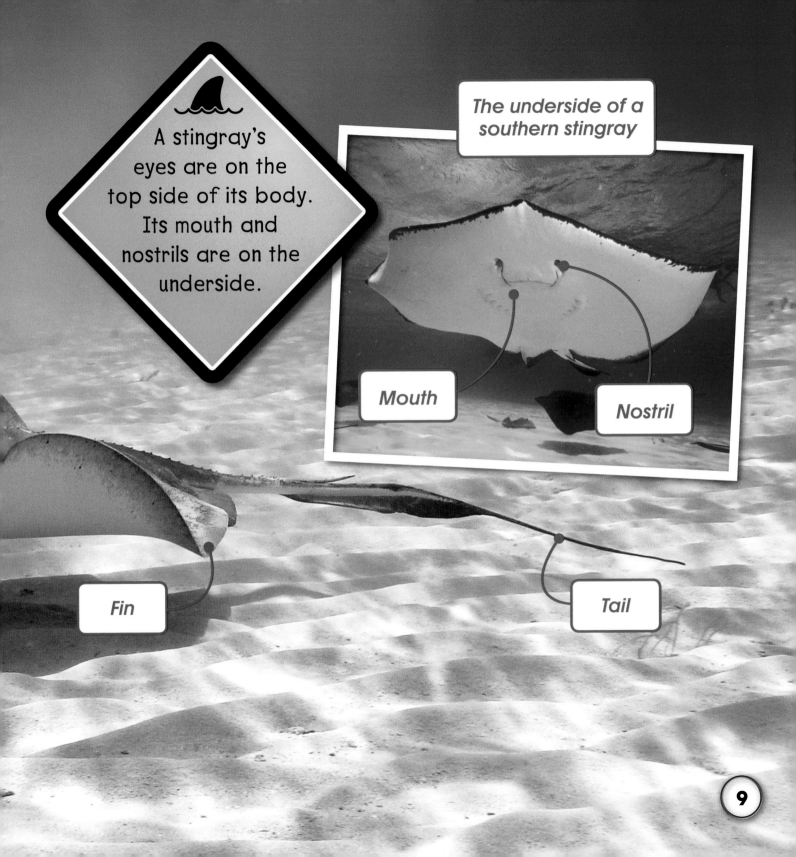

A stingray's eyes are on the top side of its body. Its mouth and nostrils are on the underside.

The underside of a southern stingray

Mouth

Nostril

Fin

Tail

A DEADLY WEAPON

A stingray's long, whip-like tail is armed with a deadly weapon known as a sting, or spine.

The sting is a razor-sharp spine, like the point of a spear. It is made from cartilage and grows from the stingray's tail, a little like a long fingernail. The edges of the spine are serrated, like the edges of a saw, with small, sharp barbs.

The sting with its vicious barbed edge can inflict a terrible wound, but that's not all it can do. The sting contains a part called a gland that produces venom. As the sting sinks into the victim's flesh, venom flows into the wound, poisoning any creature that the stingray has attacked.

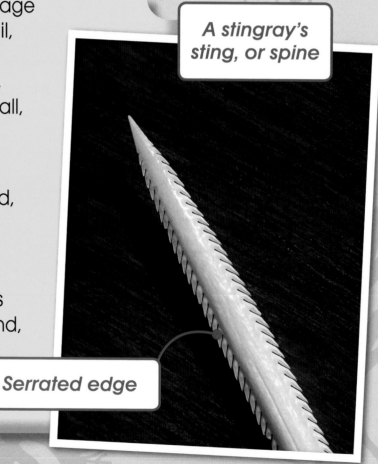

A stingray's sting, or spine

Serrated edge

Sting, or spine

A stingray's tail

A large stingray's venomous sting may be 14 inches (36 cm) long.

USING THE STING

When a stingray needs to use its sting, it faces its victim and flips its long tail over its body. Then it strikes, sinking its sting into its victim's flesh.

Stingrays may have a deadly weapon, but they do not actively attack other animals. Stingrays only use their stings to defend themselves if they are attacked by a predator such as a shark or a larger ray.

Many people are afraid of stingrays, believing they want to attack people, but this is not true. Very occasionally, a stingray might sting a person. The animal only does this, however, if it is startled by a swimmer or diver and believes it is in danger.

A large stingray is powerful enough to drive its sharp sting through the side of a wooden boat!

Tail

Sting

13

STINGRAYS AND PEOPLE

As the venom from a stingray sting enters the flesh, it causes terrible pain.

Removing a sting is also damaging because the barbs on its edges point backward. The sharp sting may enter the victim's body smoothly, but pulling the barbed sting back out again is agonizing.

Most attacks on humans by stingrays happen when people accidentally step on a stingray that is hidden under the sand. Then the panicked animal attacks in self-defense.

When walking in waters where stingrays are known to live, swimmers should slowly shuffle their feet through the sand. This gentle movement will disturb a stingray by touching the side of its body. Then the animal can make its escape.

The sharp point of the sting enters smoothly.

The barbs tear at flesh as the sting is pulled out.

A sting from a stingray causes a painful wound, but human deaths from stingray stings are very rare.

A stingray hidden in sand

HUNTING AND EATING

Stingrays hunt on the seabed for animals such as crabs, clams, oysters, mussels, and shrimp.

Because a stingray's eyes are on top of its body, and the creatures it is hunting are usually underneath it on the seabed, a stingray can't see its prey. To find its meal, a stingray uses special organs around its mouth. These organs are able to sense, or pick up, electrical charges. All living things give off small amounts of natural electricity. As the stingray moves over the seabed or rocks, its sensory organs detect electrical charges given off by its prey. Once the stingray senses another animal, it grabs the prey with its mouth.

Many types of stingray have sections of hard material called plates in their mouths for crushing the shells of animals such as crabs.

A crab

A stingray hunting for prey

Mussels

Clams

LITTLE STINGRAYS

Many species of fish lay eggs. Others, including stingrays, give birth to live babies. A female stingray usually gives birth to young once a year.

Baby stingrays begin their development inside eggs inside their mother. Then the babies hatch from the eggs and continue to grow and develop inside their mother's body.

A female stingray may give birth to just one or two babies, or as many as 13 at one time. The baby stingrays, known as pups, look exactly like tiny versions of their mother. As soon as they are born, the pups are able to find food and take care of themselves.

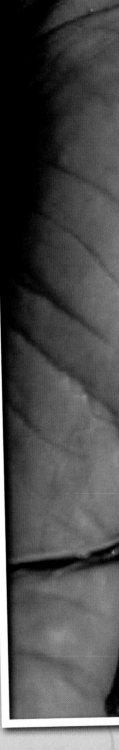

A stingray pup

A stingray can live to be 25 years old.

THE GIANT STINGRAY

The giant freshwater stingray is one of the world's largest freshwater fish.

These enormous creatures are known to live in rivers in northern Australia, New Guinea, Borneo, and Thailand. While scientists know very little about this species of stingray, people who spend time on the rivers where these fish make their homes have plenty of stories to tell. People have reported seeing giant freshwater stingrays that are 20 feet (6 m) long. A stingray of this size could weigh more than 1,000 pounds (450 kg).

There are even stories of anglers hooking a giant stingray and then having their boat dragged for miles (km) along the river by the huge creature!

The giant freshwater stingray is brown or gray and has a long tail like its ocean-dwelling cousins.

A giant freshwater stingray

CATCHING A GIANT

Zeb Hogan is a biologist who has spent time searching for and studying the world's biggest fish.

In March 2008, Zeb received a call to tell him that some anglers had caught a giant freshwater stingray in the Mekong River in Thailand. When Zeb arrived on the scene, he found the anglers holding onto a giant stingray that was 14 feet (4.3 m) long. What was even more amazing was that the stingray had just given birth to a dinner plate-sized stingray pup.

Zeb was able to study and photograph the mega fish. Then the huge mother stingray and her pup were set free to swim back into the river.

No one knows how many giant freshwater stingrays exist. In many places where they live, giant stingrays have been **overfished** and their numbers may be very low.

Zeb Hogan with the giant stingray

MEET THE FAMILY: MANTA RAYS

The manta ray may not have a deadly stinging tail like its stingray cousin, but its enormous size easily earns it the title of a real life sea monster.

Manta rays have huge triangular fins that are known as wings. The wingspan of an adult manta ray can be 23 feet (7 m) from wing tip to wing tip.

Manta rays are not predatory hunters but **plankton** feeders. As they swim, these huge animals feed on **microscopic** ocean creatures that are drifting in the water.

A female manta ray usually gives birth to just one pup at a time. The newborn baby has a wingspan of 5 feet (1.5 m)!

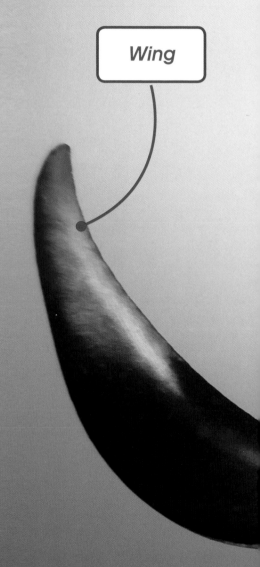

Wing

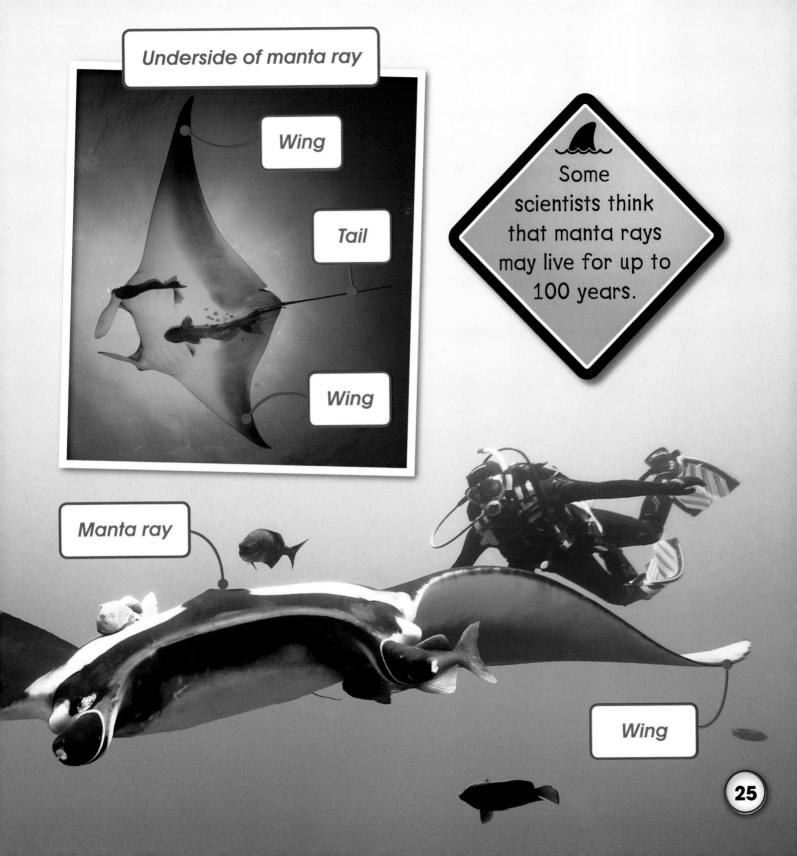

Underside of manta ray

Wing

Tail

Wing

Some scientists think that manta rays may live for up to 100 years.

Manta ray

Wing

MEET THE FAMILY: ELECTRIC RAYS

Swimming slowly along the seabed, these members of the ray family look innocent enough. The bodies of electric rays, however, can actually produce electric shocks!

The electric shock is generated by two organs inside the ray's body. The shocks can be used to stun prey and make it easier to catch or kill prey, and to give predators a warning to stay away.

While the shock produced by some rays is mild, the Atlantic torpedo ray attacks its prey with an electrifying 220 volts. That's the same amount of voltage that is running through the electrical wires in your home to power the stove or clothes dryer!

An electric ray

In ancient Greece, electric shocks from electric rays were used as a type of **anesthetic** to deaden the pain of operations and childbirth.

UP-CLOSE WITH STINGRAYS

Stingrays may have a deadly weapon, but they are gentle animals that often approach swimmers and divers.

At Stingray City, on the coast of the Cayman Islands in the Caribbean Sea, people can swim with wild stingrays. Here, there is a shallow area of ocean where fishermen would once anchor their boats to clean and cut up the fish they'd caught. The fish guts and other unwanted parts were thrown overboard. In time, stingrays learned it was a good place to find plenty of food.

Stingrays still gather in this area today, and they have become comfortable with human visitors. Now, divers and swimmers can give the animals food and have the chance to be close to these graceful, wild creatures.

Scuba divers
say that stingrays
often swim close to them
as if the animals are investigating
the strange human creatures
that are visiting
their ocean
habitat.

Divers get up-close with stingrays at Stingray City.

GLOSSARY

anesthetic (a-nis-THEH-tik)
A drug that is used to numb a body part or put an animal or person to sleep during an operation or medical procedure.

biologist (by-AH-luh-jist)
A scientist who studies animals, plants, and other living things.

cartilage (KAR-tuh-lij)
Strong, rubbery tissue found in the bodies of many animals. Humans have cartilage in their noses and ears.

fish (FISH)
Cold-blooded animals that live in water. Fish breathe through gills and have a skeleton. Most fish lay eggs.

freshwater (FRESH-wah-ter)
Water in streams, rivers, ponds, and some lakes that does not contain salt.

habitat (HA-buh-tat)
The place where an animal or plant normally lives. A habitat may be a forest, the ocean, or a backyard.

microscopic (my-kruh-SKAH-pik)
Too small to be seen with a person's eyes and only visible through a microscope.

overfished (oh-vur-FISHT)
Decreased in numbers when too many of a species have been caught by people and the animal is in danger of dying out.

plankton (PLANGK-tun)
Microscopic animals and plants that float in open water in oceans.

predators (PREH-duh-terz)
Animals that hunt and kill other animals for food.

predatory (PREH-duh-tor-ee)
Living by hunting and eating other animals.

prey (PRAY)
An animal that is hunted by another animal as food.

sea serpents (SEE SUR-pents)
Huge, ocean-dwelling monsters, often with long, armlike tentacles, that appear in old stories.

species (SPEE-sheez)
One type of living thing. The members of a species look alike and can produce young together.

venom (VEH-num)
A poison that is injected into a victim by a sting or bite.

READ MORE

Miller, Tori. *Manta Rays*. Freaky Fish. New York: PowerKids Press, 2009.

Niver, Heather Moore. *20 Fun Facts About Stingrays*. Fun Fact File: Fierce Fish. New York: Gareth Stevens, 2013.

Rake, Jody Sullivan. *Rays*. Mankato, MN: Capstone Press, 2007.

INDEX